Little воок
of Balm for the
Broken Soul

To Oscar,

From one writer to another!
Keep on writing and inspiring!
Clare.

WRITTEN BY
Clare Francis-Slater

ILLUSTRATED BY
Lynne Hollingsworth

Conscious Dreams
PUBLISHING

First Printed in United Kingdom 2023

Published by Conscious Dreams Publishing
www.consciousdreamspublishing.com

Edited by Lee Dickinson, Daniella Blechner and Elise Abram

Cover Design and Illustrations by Lynne Hollingsworth

Typeset by Oksana Kosovan

ISBN: 978-1-915522-36-8

Dedication

This book is dedicated to...

Dr Kirsty V Williams (Highly Specialised Lead Clinical Psychologist Cancer and Palliative Medicine), Royal Derby Hospital, who was instrumental in helping me gently heal from my trauma, look at my experience with fresh eyes, and be kinder to myself.

And my family, for being my rock in the storm.

Contents

The journey of 1,000 steps begins
with a single step, so let's take that first
step together and begin.

Preface

I am writing this book in the hope it will one day help others who may find themselves in a similar situation to mine.

Following my breast cancer treatment, I experienced a state of poor mental health and had to learn to be gentle with myself to get better. After that, I experienced what is called "post-traumatic growth", which is a positive psychological change that some individuals experience after a life crisis or traumatic event. This transformative positive mental shift was life-changing, and with it came many life lessons I would like to share with you in this book.

In the spring of 2018, I discovered that I had breast cancer. Luckily, I found my lump early. It was treatable with a small operation and some radiotherapy. I felt as if I was sailing through what I thought would be the worst of it.

By the winter of 2018, I was a shadow of my former self, tearful every day, listless and lacking energy for everyday tasks, and tired and overwhelmed by life itself. Even the smallest of tasks felt unmanageable. I was anxious and woke every morning with a sense of dread about how I would get through the day. I avoided social contact as much as possible, apart from my immediate family. I lost all of my confidence and hope. It was an emotionally exhausting, painful, and worrying time. I wondered how I would ever get out of the hole I had fallen into.

So, what happened? What went so wrong? Why did I feel so bad?

As I said, my treatment went well, and the cancer was fortunately gone, but I felt so different. I coped with my treatment by continuing to work full-time. I'm a primary school teacher, and I kept myself busy with work and family. I remember my husband asking me, 'How will we cope?'

I responded, 'We'll just carry on as normal,' and we did.

It worked for a while. It got us through the worst of the worry and the early days of not knowing if I would be okay or not. As a coping mechanism, I put it out of my mind and chose not to think about it. I even did a parents' evening on the same day I got my cancer diagnosis!

By the autumn of that same year, it had started to catch up with me. I think it was delayed shock at the fact that I had stared death in the face, and I was only forty-one years old.

The tamoxifen tablets the doctors put me on didn't suit me at all. They sent me into a sort of early menopause: I had hot flushes, was anxious, and was so tearful. My oestrogen levels suddenly dropped due to my medication. It affected me so badly that I could not continue to teach, as I burst into tears at school over nothing and did not know why. It was so distressing. With the support of my consultant, I was off the tamoxifen by mid-January but then had to wait months for it to get fully out of my system. Then I had to get myself out of the deep hole I had fallen into.

Even though revisiting my feelings during the writing of this book has, at times, been hard, forcing me to remember that tough period of my life has also been a cathartic process. This is a positive book that shows you ways you can help yourself to feel better at those low moments when it can sometimes seem too hard to carry on. You may find my story relatable and very honest. I will share with you how I got better and that it is possible to get better with the right help.

There are so many positives from that traumatic time that now I can clearly see that I am on the other side of it all. I went on an amazing journey of self-discovery, which was long and painful, to begin with, but it was also enlightening, fulfilling, and enriching. I am now even more honest, accepting, and so much kinder to myself. I feel better equipped to deal with tough times, everyday life, and its challenges.

Although my post-traumatic growth experience came about after my breast cancer diagnosis and treatment, I feel that the ideas in this book are applicable to anyone who is or has recently experienced any sort of trauma in their lives.

I hope that *The Little Book of Balm* will act as a beacon of hope, shining a light to guide you in the darkest of times. It is not intended to be clever or full of fancy phrases; rather it's written simply and plainly to help support you through tough times. Think of this book as a friend talking to you, offering comfort when you may feel lost and unsure about which way to turn. The words of advice I share are from my heart and my own lived experience. I do not claim to have all the answers, but I hope my strategies will help. Many of the ideas within *The Little Book of Balm* came to me when out walking, either alone or with a friend, in the beautiful fields and hills of rural Amber Valley in Derbyshire, where I live, or when I settled inside for a long chat with a good friend over a hot cuppa.

I do hope that *The Little Book of Balm* will give you some fresh perspectives and helpful hints and provide solace and comfort like a balm for your broken soul.

At the end of the book, there are a couple of blank pages for you to jot down your own thoughts and reflections to support you on your journey. What resonated with you in the chapter? What changes might you make? How might you be kinder to yourself?

Read this book if you want to help yourself but are not sure where to start. Think of this little book as a survival kit, a backpack you can reach for if you ever find yourself falling and don't know when it will end or how you will get back up. It is full of coping strategies, life lessons, gems of positive wisdom, eternal truths, helpful thoughts, and most of all...HOPE!

CHAPTER 1

Focus on the Basics

I t sounds simple, but it is amazing how effective focusing on the basics can be; eating and sleeping well are so important. It is also important to always take care of ourselves. When we go through particularly tough times in life, this advice becomes even more important. With a well-nourished body and a well-rested mind, you'll stand a much better chance of coping with life's ups and downs in the day ahead. You'll even be able to get your life back on track when it throws you a curveball.

A healthy, fit, well-functioning body is so important. In the autumn of 2018, I had some blood tests done as

I was feeling exhausted, and I knew something wasn't right. My tiredness reminded me of how I felt while pregnant with my first child, so I suspected that my iron and vitamin D levels were low. As it turned out, my iron and vitamin D levels were seriously deficient, so it was no wonder I felt exhausted. My doctor put me on super-strength iron and vitamin D tablets, and I felt a real lift in my energy levels. I continue to take daily vitamin tablets, including iron and vitamin D, as they keep me feeling strong and well.

When I felt at my lowest on an emotional and physical level, even starting the day was a struggle. I noticed that, in the mornings, once I had woken up, a pattern of excessive rumination set in every day in which I lay in bed, worrying about how I was going to face the day ahead. The days seemed so long when they stretched out ahead of me, and I needed to try to 'get through' them. The sense of dread and impending doom was awful. My mind ran away from me, spiralling down.

A Helpful Hint

A lovely, helpful friend suggested that when I wake up, it would be better to get up to help put a stop to the negative thoughts and ruminations in my mind. I gave it a go, and it really helped me to start the day better. Rather than lying awake in the morning, thinking and worrying about negative thoughts, I'd get up (although I didn't feel like it) and potter around the house quietly before everyone else woke up. This gentle, 'active' start to the day was much better, and it helped stop the rumination and generalised anxiety I experienced in the mornings; I distracted myself. Without really knowing it, I was retraining my brain to focus on something else and slowly getting back into the driving seat in my head.

Take care of yourself; it's a form of healing and self-love. You deserve it. Treat yourself as you would a good friend.

CHAPTER 2

It's Okay Not to be Okay

Since when in Western society did we place an expectation on the human experience that we should feel happy all the time? It's completely unrealistic. Sadness and unhappiness are a part of our natural range of human responses to our lived situations.

After my cancer treatment finished, I felt a profound sense of sadness that my body had somehow 'failed' me, 'let me down' because I'd become poorly. In my post-treatment support, I learned that this was quite a common reaction after a cancer diagnosis or treatment.

We can also experience a sense of mistrust for our own bodies when they go 'wrong' in a different way. For example, I had a similar feeling of sadness when I couldn't have a natural birth with my first daughter. It didn't go as expected at all. I had planned for a natural birth with my first daughter — a home birth with a birthing pool — but it ended up being the most medicalised, intervention-led birth experience (disappointing, but completely necessary) when I was blue-lighted to our local hospital on the night of her birth. I was later left with post-traumatic stress disorder due to the extreme stress of the experience, post-natal depression when the tiredness kicked in, and a feeling of 'failure' because I hadn't been able to give birth naturally as I had so wanted.

Of course, the most important thing was that Amelia, our beautiful daughter, and I were fit and well, but at the same time and for a long time after, I felt scared and saddened that my body hadn't done what it was meant to do. It hadn't done what I had felt was the most natural thing in the world: give birth on my own. I was gutted.

However, this feeling lessened with time. Time is a great healer. There is nothing wrong with feeling sad, but when we fight against the feeling of sadness, it feels worse. I had to learn to allow myself to feel sad. It was okay to feel sad. Feeling a 'negative' emotion like sadness is uncomfortable, but if we sit with the sadness, as my mum always says, 'it will pass'. If you feel bad about feeling sad, then it's double the trouble! Feelings of guilt can creep in, and it's a downward spiral.

Instead, recognise the feeling of sadness, unhappiness, whatever it is you feel sad about. Acknowledge it and learn to sit with it and accept it. That's the hardest part—I talk more about that later in this book.

At this time, it's important to let go of the language that puts pressure on ourselves, like 'must', 'should', 'need to', and so on. Learn to be kinder to yourself, and try to unburden yourself from these unnecessary pressures.

We all wear many 'hats' in our lives. My hats are mum, wife, daughter, sister, teacher, and friend; however, at my lowest ebb, I was unable to function in any of my usual roles. It was all I could do to get through each day. All I could focus on was trying to get myself well again. It's like in the aeroplane safety message when they tell you to put your own mask on first. Sometimes in life, we have to do this, and that's okay.

It took me some time to stop feeling guilty about not 'being there' for my family and children. Although I was there physically, I was not there mentally for a while.

With support, I realised that, over the years, I had built up an image of my 'preferred' self that was always on top of life and positive, a coper who could take care of my children and run the home, do my job, and contribute financially to the pot. I put a lot of pressure on myself to be good at what I did. I took pride in doing what I did well. On some level, I thought the house would fall apart without my being an intrinsic part of it.

Well, guess what? It didn't! I underestimated what my husband and children were capable of, and subconsciously, this put pressure on me to try to do it all. I used to tell myself that I had to do everything, and only I could do it *'properly'*. I also had to let go of aiming for 'perfect'. Striving for something unattainable is a waste of time and ultimately exhausting. Good is good enough.

A Helpful Hint

Due to this stressful and unhappy phase, I gradually lost my appetite, which is something that always happens when I feel stressed. If I'm not relaxed, I don't feel hungry, I can't think what I'd like to eat or cook, and the cycle continues, but with a young and growing family, meals must be put on the table each day.

To a very large extent, my lovely husband, Ben, stepped up and cooked for all of us for a long while. I shared this 'problem' of my loss of appetite due to stress with my psychologist friend, and she suggested a helpful idea: to create a family meal plan as a family exercise. She suggested that each family member select a meal they wanted in the weekly meal plan (within reason—I didn't plan to cook lobster once a week!). That way, we would all take joint ownership of it. Putting meals on the table each day is basically an operational thing, so we started treating it as such. The family meal plan was helpful because we would know what needed buying each week, and what to cook didn't need to be thought about or decided upon each night (a pressure in itself after a long day at work!)—we would just cook what was on the plan. Of course, the plan would be a flexible thing, so we could swap the meals around as it suited us.

This took a huge pressure off of mealtimes for me, and it helped me re-engage with cooking and relax enough to enjoy eating my meals again, but on a new 'shared' footing, which felt so much better.

CHAPTER 3

Seek Support

Sometimes when we are unwell, we need some help to get better. We can't do it alone. Sometimes it's hard to know where to get the right help. Sometimes friends and family are enough, and sometimes they are not. Sometimes professional support is needed. It's okay; there is no shame in it. Get the help you need.

Each person's situation when they are at a low ebb is personal to them. What is right for one isn't necessarily right for another. Getting better isn't a one-size-fits-all approach, but as I guide you through my book, you will see there are many things you can do to help yourself in tough times.

In the first instance, when I realised I wasn't well enough to work, I went with my husband to see our family GP. She listened and agreed that I wasn't well enough to work; I was an emotional and physical wreck. I felt as though I'd been steamrolled by life and had no reserves left. I discovered my cancer at Easter, was treated over the summer, went back to work in September, and by the Christmas holidays, had crashed and burned.

After signing me off from work, she advised me to 'Eat, sleep well, and take some moderate exercise.' I did that for a couple of weeks, but with no improvement in my mood, she suggested anti-depressants. I didn't feel as if that was the right course of action for me. No judgement at all on others—and I know many other people that they have really helped—but I just didn't feel it was what I wanted or needed at the time.

I felt like I felt that way physically and emotionally for a reason. Although I didn't know how or when I would get better (I still hoped I would, at some point, feel better), I knew that when I did, I wanted to be sure I was *actually* better and that my body and mind had recovered. Although I genuinely suffered in my head and body (aches and pains associated with poor mental health), I didn't want a pill to mask the pain so I would know when I had really healed. Having said that, I would not want to suggest that anyone should make any sudden changes in their medication without consulting their doctor. The decision I made was based on my circumstances, and after consultation with my doctor, it was agreed that I could find my own way to get better slowly. Each person and their situation are so individual and should be treated as such.

I always remember that my husband's grandma said, when her lovely, gentle husband died, that she 'needed to feel the pain of grieving' so she could process it properly. Grieving after a loved one has died is a normal and natural response to death and loss, and we need to sit with that uncomfortable emotion and not judge it. We need to just be in it, and in time, we learn to live with the feeling.

I'm an open, friendly, and sociable person, so a part of my healing process was to open up and be honest about my emotions. I generally do wear my heart on my sleeve with people I am close to.

In doing so, I found some wonderful support. Some might think it was found in unlikely places in these modern times as we are accustomed to living more and more individually. Within my local community, I found a group of my nearest and dearest neighbours — some widowed, some divorced, all ladies ranging from their fifties to nineties — who were like a sisterhood. They all offered me a shoulder to cry on and a kind word of advice in my hours of need. They wrapped their arms around me and accepted me in my most vulnerable state, which was like a balm that helped heal my open wounds.

Opening up and sharing during a chance conversation on the way to dropping off or picking up my kids at school helped me, but I noticed that sometimes, it also seemed to help others, too. When I took off my 'mask' that everything was okay in my world, they took off theirs, and within five minutes, we were deep in conversation, dabbing tears from our eyes. Being able to share our emotions (with carefully selected friends, not all and sundry!) can be a deeply healing human experience, as we can see our common humanity. We see that we are all vulnerable at times, and we all have some big and challenging emotions to deal with, but together, we can help each other deal with these trying times in our lives. We can support one another; we are *not* alone!

As I went on this journey of healing, I also learned that sometimes, the people who are closest to you are not necessarily the people best placed to help you. That is not to say that they don't want to help or they don't love you; they just might not have experienced any of the feelings you are experiencing. Or, as much as you love them and they love you, they may not have the emotional language or toolkit to support you. They may also have their own 'emotional baggage', and therefore, do not have the capacity to support you when you want them to. Learning to accept this helps, as does knowing that they love you and it's not their fault they can't help you. Also, some people are so close to you that it's painful for them to see you suffer, and they just want you to be like your old self. People who you are close to, those that do find themselves unable to support you on an emotional level, will probably find their own way of helping in a different way. Some of my family members found they were best able to be supportive in a more practical way with meals and baking, which was a helpful and lovely way to show they cared.

When you reach out, you will find that other people will come into your life that can help you through these tough times. I feel very lucky to live in a small rural village where a lot of people know each other, or at least a lot of faces are familiar. It's so easy to connect with people in my village that I rarely walk anywhere without stopping to talk to someone I bump into, which I love! I realise how important it is that we are connected—isolation isn't good for us, especially when we struggle mentally.

I was fortunate to have received some specialist mental health support in various forms to help me get better when I was unwell. The specialist support made an enormous difference in my recovery.

I was lucky to have received a lot of support from my work initially, and then some support was organised through my doctor. I had an occupational health session, some talk therapy, equine therapy, and expert professional psychological support from a fabulous experienced psychologist in the NHS who was dealing with cancer patients and the mental fallout they experienced, either at the point of diagnosis or following treatment. She was truly amazing! Every time I went to see her, I came away feeling a little more restored and a little stronger. I feel so lucky to have been referred to her.

My treatment started in the autumn of 2018 with occupational health as I desperately tried to hold onto the teaching role I had. It ended with expert NHS psychological support from May to December 2019. I am profoundly grateful for all the support I received; I know how fortunate I was to get it. I am very aware that many people may not be as fortunate. Each part of the professional support helped me get slowly better properly and at my own pace. I learned so much about myself on that journey that helped me to understand myself better: my thoughts, feelings, and reactions to situations. I learned how to cope better now and in the future, and I am sharing the lessons I learned along my journey with you now.

For anyone else in the pits of despair, falling and falling and not knowing when they'll stop (which is so scary) — there is hope. There is always hope. You will get better with the right support. You can get better again. Trust me.

A Helpful Hint

Seek support when you need it. Don't feel ashamed to ask for help. I think it's actually a strength to recognise that something is not right. Acknowledge it and seek the support you need, whether informal or professional.

CHAPTER 4

Let Go

Sometimes, things happen in our lives that make us realise we are not in control. Living in the UK, we don't usually experience natural disasters like earthquakes or hurricanes. I'm talking about things like health scares, accidents, the death of a loved one — both family and pets, losing our jobs, and so on.

> "Life is what happens to you while you're busy
> making other plans."
> — *Allen Saunders/John Lennon*

It can be a scary realisation that we are out of control when something 'bad' happens. This can induce feelings of anxiety, general fear, and panic; I felt this. I felt as though the rug had been pulled out from underneath me. It's a normal, common reaction, but it's uncomfortable. At that point, my lovely psychologist told me to try to learn that it's okay not to be in control and to accept it, so I gradually learned to let go. It was quite liberating! It's exhausting trying to control everything all the time.

Bringing up children is a busy, full-on job and at times you can feel stretched to your limits, especially when you throw work into the mix too. In the early years, you are finding your way and learning by your mistakes, what works and what doesn't. And as parents you both are bringing your own early experiences and have your own ideas of how things should be done. In all matters, including the children, I was quite particular, and small things would matter to me. For example, we could end up in a 'heated discussion' over whether or not it really mattered if the children wore wellies on a wet day. I felt as if that mattered a lot, and I was quite passionate about them being dressed appropriately for the weather, while my husband thought it wasn't important. It's how we differ; I am quite exacting and my husband has a more laisse-faire approach to life. Perhaps, this was a part of my 'perfectionism', that I liked everything done well, and I felt there was a 'right' way and a 'wrong/not so good' way. It was a thorn in our relationship and a source of irritation and distress for both of us, but I suppose it's not uncommon in the early years of bringing up a family when both of you have different ideas of what's 'best'. It's something we have to work through as we adjust and learn to compromise. In the end, in this particular situation, I think I acquiesced. I decided it was more important that the children were going out and having fun with their dad, it wasn't worth fighting about what they were wearing on their feet!

After a trauma or stressful experience, it's natural to feel fearful and frightened. As human beings, we always want to feel safe, so after a trauma, you may react like I did and have a desperate desire to try to get back to that feeling of safety (how we used to feel prior to the trauma). We all react differently to traumatic experiences. Some try to nullify the fearful feeling and stress with an overreliance on something that temporarily eases the painful feelings, such as alcohol, over-eating, drugs, and the like.

Some may develop obsessive-compulsive disorder (OCD), and try to overly control everything in their lives and the lives of those around them in a desperate attempt to feel safe and in control again. When we feel in control of our lives, we also feel safe.

I fell into another group when I was trying to go back to the 'old me', the one before I had the cancer diagnosis and the trauma. My psychologist explained to me that 'me' didn't exist anymore, and I couldn't go back to how I was as I had changed after having that experience. My desire to return to the 'old' me was causing me pain and emotional suffering, and it jarred me that I was unable to do it.

I remember a powerful session I once had with my equine therapist. Equine therapists use horses to enable the client to connect with their emotions and release their trauma. She told me to hold onto the reins of my therapeutic horse, George, and imagine that George was my cancer. I then had to walk around the manège and 'take my cancer with me'. She said I must do it to be able to move on with my life. She cleverly and clearly demonstrated to me that my cancer was now a part of my life story — my story. I couldn't pretend it hadn't happened as much as I wanted to, on many different levels. I had to take it with me and accept that it had happened. It was so hard to walk George around the manège. He didn't want to go, nor did I want to take him. I had tears streaming down my face as I tried to get George to move. Although it was a very emotional exercise, it felt painful and uncomfortable, but it was also helpful as it made me realise that I had to do it. I learned that no matter how hard it was to get moving, I had to find a way to go forward, taking my cancer with me. I had to move on physically and mentally, no matter how hard it was. In time, I was also taught how to see how I had grown as a person, having had this experience, and fortunately survived it.

A Helpful Hint

If/when we have a deeply traumatic experience in our lives, a time of extreme stress, once it is over, try to accept that it has happened and mourn any loss. Don't judge yourself; let your emotions come and go and wash over you. Learn what you can from the experience, take any positives, and grow out of it like a phoenix rising from the ashes. Come back anew, stronger, and more resilient. We all have our favourite quotes or mottos we live by, this is one my dad always used to say:

> "That which does not kill us only serves
> to make us stronger."
> — *German philosopher Friedrich Wilhelm Nietzsche*

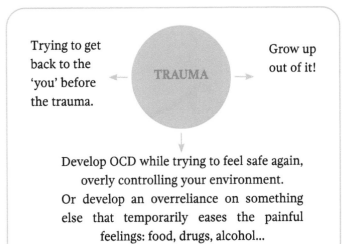

Trying to get back to the 'you' before the trauma.

TRAUMA

Grow up out of it!

Develop OCD while trying to feel safe again, overly controlling your environment.
Or develop an overreliance on something else that temporarily eases the painful feelings: food, drugs, alcohol...

CHAPTER 5

Nourish

S elf-care has become a bit of a buzz term these days; we hear a lot about it. As a result, it has also become a booming industry, with spas popping up all over the place and the notion of 'me' or 'alone' time becoming more common.

I think there are a lot of truths in the benefits of taking the time to nourish yourself while filling your metaphorical 'cup' or 'bucket'. It is always time well spent that will pay you back in dividends.

There is a timeless children's picture book called Have you Filled a Bucket Today? It was written by Carol McCloud in 2006. I have shared this story with many children over the years as it is a helpful visual way to understand how our happiness works. The story is built on the idea that we all carry an invisible bucket around with us that holds our good thoughts and feelings about ourselves. A full bucket means you feel happy; an empty bucket signifies sadness or loneliness. It explains how we can be 'bucket fillers' with our kind actions or 'bucket dippers' with our unkind actions or words. Also, when you 'fill someone else's bucket', you also automatically fill your own (i.e., if you make someone else happy, you feel happy, too), and if you 'dip into someone else's bucket', not only do you empty their bucket, but you empty your own bucket, too. That is to say that if you make someone else unhappy, you make yourself feel unhappy, too. I believe there are some valuable lessons in the story about the power of being kind, for children and adults alike, and these lessons shouldn't be underestimated. We would all benefit from more kindness in our world.

Take a moment, breath in and out deeply, and take some time to think about what brings you joy. What makes you feel happy? The truth is that when you have not really been feeling yourself for a while, this is sometimes quite a difficult exercise. I remember feeling as if I hadn't felt that 'spark' of joy for so long; I almost couldn't remember what made me feel happy! It was a really scary realisation. Of course, I never stopped loving my family, but because I was so low, I had entered this strange, emotionally detached phase in which I wasn't able to connect as I was once able to; I didn't feel the joy.

A Helpful Hint

It was suggested to me that I should get a large sheet of paper or use the back of some old wallpaper and jot down anything I could think of that made me feel happy or good. This is a very personal and unique experience — what floats your boat is special to you. I remember writing a lot of different random thoughts on my mind map, whatever came into my head, such as seeing friends, writing, walking, nature, gardening, singing and dancing, dogs, family, hot baths, swimming, and so on.

Once you've identified what makes you feel happy and alive, do it often. Even if it is just five minutes of doing something you like, it can be enough to lift your mood a little and fill your cup. Aim to do something that brings you joy every day. This is not a luxury — it's essential. Do whatever it is that relights any kind of spark deep within you. It may be imperceptible at first, but over time, the transformative effect this has is amazing. It will lift you up, little by little. Don't ever feel guilty about spending time doing something that makes you feel good, as it will make you a happier, more fulfilled, relaxed, and more content you. Plus, you will be better placed to support your friends, family, and those around you if your cup is full rather than empty. Your happiness will spread happiness when you become a bucket-filler rather than a bucket-dipper.

With our busy lives and the many demands on our time and energy — work commitments, family, children, running a busy home and all that entails — we need to give ourselves a break. Taking some time out to restore and replenish ourselves is time well spent. The time we take to fill our cups will pay us back in bucket loads, and you will feel more energy and generally more resilient to cope with the ups and downs of everyday life.

I have always loved walking. Having grown up in the countryside with a dog, walking has always been a part of my life, so I benefitted hugely from regular walks in the countryside where we live or pottering around in my garden. Relaxed meals with my family and daily, long, really hot soaks in the bath were my simple pleasures. The hot, soapy, sweet-smelling water was a tonic to my body and mind and a massive part of my recovery process. It gave me time every day to relax during a stressful time, and that was exactly what my body and mind cried out for. I also got into a daily routine of a little gentle stretching, which I found beneficial. I often find that simple things — the ones that money can't buy — are the best.

Another Helpful Hint

Another helpful thought my equine therapist shared with me one time as we were walking around the manège with George was to 'remember [that] we are called human beings [and] not human doings'. What she meant by this was that in modern Western society, we attach so much value to being productive. The busier we are, the better we feel about ourselves. We connect our businesses with our self-importance, and it's how we give ourselves value, but it's actually an unhelpful idea with regard to our mental health. It's true that I get a buzz from being busy and active, and it's good to have that at times in our lives, but as human beings, we benefit from striking a good balance of being busy and 'down-time'; time just 'being' and not doing. I thought this was an interesting point, and I try to remember this whenever I feel the need to always be 'productive'.

CHAPTER 6

Time, Space and Baby Steps

I remember that, when I was feeling low, I was desperate to get better quickly. I was suffering, and it was emotionally painful. I wanted this bad feeling to end and to get on with my life again. I remember having a conversation with my GP, and she said it might take some time to pass, perhaps months, maybe even a year. I was so shocked at the timeframe she put on my recovery process; I couldn't believe it might take that long. In the end, it wasn't that long, but I think she was trying to help me to get a more long-term view of the process of getting better and to allow myself the time to heal and be restored slowly, gently, and at my own pace.

I wasn't helping myself by putting pressure on myself to get better and feel better quickly. Conversely, when I was able to take the pressure off of myself, it quite possibly helped me heal and feel better as I wasn't jarring against my emotions and feelings but accepting them. By accepting them, I moved closer to getting better little by little, rather than rallying against the state I was in.

'It will pass' became one of my mum's favourite sayings to us throughout our childhood for any given situation, happy or sad. I kept reminding myself of this saying during this time.

As the wonderful writer Maya Angelou once said, 'Every storm runs out of rain.' Tough times don't last forever. Give yourself time to take stock, and stop if you need to. Reassess where you are and where you are going. Perhaps you could do with making changes, but be careful not to make any large, hasty changes when you're not in a good place emotionally and mentally.

Getting better and feeling better certainly doesn't happen overnight, especially when you've been spiralling into a dark hole for so long. It takes time to come up out of it.

Dr Peter Harvey said that, 'the process of self recovery comes in stops and starts, you may feel like you are taking two steps forward and one back. But each time your mood lifts it lifts a little higher, and each setback is a little shorter until we find ourselves feeling better and able to look back on what we came through.'

I certainly felt this when coming out of my low ebb. I also remember the sense of mild panic and worry each time I had a little setback in my energy levels and mood. For example, I might start to feel a little lighter in my heart and not quite as downcast and have a glimmer of hope and a general feeling of being uplifted, but that would be followed by waking up the next morning without the lighter, hopeful feeling. That led me to worry about what might be happening, the 'Oh, no! I'm not getting better; I feel bad again!' panic.

That was a really hard time. I was ever watchful of my mood and energy levels and hypersensitive to a dip in either. I remember being so focused on checking in on my mood. Every day I'd ask myself, 'How am I feeling?' at several points in the day to see if I was okay. Constantly checking in on myself and noting any little dips as a sign that I wasn't potentially well again was a tiresome and exhausting practice as it reminded me of the exhaustion after my treatment. It was a time filled with worry and fear, including the fear that the cancer might come back. I thought that any little lump or bump might be something dangerous. There was also the fear that I might never feel consistently good again for any length of time. Rather I'd be stuck in a 'limbo land', oscillating between occasionally being slightly okay and then not as good.

When people used to say, 'How are you?' — a casually innocuous question on the school run — I had a pre-planned answer. I didn't want to be untrue to myself, wear a mask to hide my emotions, and pretend everything was okay when it wasn't, so

I couldn't genuinely reply with 'Good, thanks! You?' even though that used to be my go-to, stock answer.

I decided that 'I'm okay' would feel more authentic for the time being. It certainly was not 'good', but it was equally not 'terrible'. I was slowly — very slowly — getting stronger, both physically and emotionally, so 'okay' was as far as I could go. It also felt like a fitting response, as I was learning to 'be okay without being okay', so okay was not lying.

Post-treatment, my psychologist gave me a really helpful pack of literature to read to help support my journey of recovery. It was about the recovery process and what one might expect. It was written in 1999 and 2002 as a series of lectures given by an eminent clinical psychologist who worked with patients post-treatment to support them with their psychological recovery after cancer. It was written in plain English, and I found it reassuring to read; it really resonated with me. Dr Peter Harvey, now retired, shared his experience while supporting patients on their painful and personal journeys after the trauma of diagnosis and treatment when, in the end, they felt exhausted, numb, wrung out, anxious, and fearful, with nothing left in the tank.

I could relate to what he shared. He talked of the stages of recovery after a trauma—any trauma—to heal and repair ourselves and that we need to go through each of the stages to build a real and lasting foundation for our emotional and physical stability. He talked of the recovery process happening in three stages: recuperation, convalescence, and rehabilitation. I found it a helpful idea that there were stages of recovery after a trauma; it made sense to me. It said in the booklet:

- **Recuperation:** a period of rest after a traumatic event to give your mind and body time to recover.
- **Convalescence:** a rather lovely, old-fashioned term with the association of rugs, the seaside, fresh air, daybeds, and strengthening broth! Sadly, its usage is in decline. Its Latin root appropriately means to 'grow strong'.

These first two stages provide the foundation and the energy to move on to the final stage:

- **Rehabilitation:** a process of regaining and refreshing old skills and learning and refining new ones to live the life you want

I found all of this information very useful, and like a guide through uncharted territory, it helped steer me through. It was something to kind of hang my hat on.

As a new way of going forward, my psychologist advised me to hold on to my plans lightly, and I really like the idea behind that phrase—nothing is set in stone, plans change, and that's okay. It has served me well these past few years, especially going through the uncertainty of the global pandemic and its effect on our everyday lives.

She also helped me to reframe the way I viewed my time off work and my recovery period, as she noticed I had attached so many negative emotions to it. I felt a sense of guilt and failure that I wasn't coping, as well as frustration and anger with myself. She suggested that I think of my time off work as a 'creative incubation', essentially a quiet time for self-reflection, when I could engage in some creative activities for their therapeutic qualities and allow positive thoughts to begin to flow. I loved the phrase *creative incubation,* and I held onto it as a helpful and positive reframing of the phase I was in. It gently encouraged me to read, explore ideas about my identity, and engage in creative writing and art, which was healing for me.

Getting to the Nub of It

If you spiral down really low, you may find that you hit what feels like 'rock bottom' (at least, it felt like that to me). I had lost all sense of hope, life felt so painful, and every day, I was in a state of mental anguish, unable to escape or get any respite from myself and my thoughts. It was torturous, and I dreaded the day ahead. I woke up each day with a sense of impending doom filled with anxiety and sadness. It was awful, and I wanted it to stop. At that point, I felt like I was such a drain on my nearest and dearest and that they would be better off without me (this is how bad having poor mental health can make you feel). Fortunately, it was a fleeting thought, but the fact that I had even thought of it scared me.

'The mind is a powerful force. It can enslave us or empower us. It can plunge us into the depths of misery or take us to the heights of ecstasy. Learn to use the power wisely.'
— *David Cuschieri*

Although it doesn't feel like it at the time, when you suffer so much and you are in such mental pain, in these darkest moments in life, there is a chance to grow. This is an opportunity to learn something more about yourself and possibly change direction if you are able to listen to your heart, that quiet little inner voice, and what it's telling you.

When we are busy getting on with our lives, we are generally blissfully unaware of our deep-seated anxieties or worries and fears. They are buried so deep, and we've developed our own coping strategies that have so far served us well, so our buried emotional baggage doesn't bother us on a day-to-day basis.

However, when times are tough, and life feels like an effort, this unresolved emotional baggage can rise to the surface. As we slowly unravel, we lie there, stripped bare. This is an uncomfortable process as it makes us feel extremely vulnerable, but there is a silver lining. If we can learn and grow from it, it can end up being an empowering and positive experience for personal growth — this is called post-traumatic growth.

CHAPTER 7

Championing Difference

Both times in my life, when I've hit a very low ebb, I've had an 'I'm different' voice in my head. At age thirty-one, I gave birth to our first child. It was a wonderful occasion, but then I entered a perfect storm of the post-traumatic stress of the birth, plus post-natal depression due to a lack of sleep and a colicky, unsettled baby. Then, ten years later, at forty-one, after my cancer treatment, I had the same 'negative' thought replaying in my head.

As a dual-heritage child—born of a British white mother and a Caribbean father and brought up in exclusively 'white' areas—I learned to blend in and assimilate as a child. I didn't focus on my differences or celebrate them; rather, I wanted to be the same as my friends (as all little children do). I was so lucky growing up—I had a very happy childhood with a loving, stable, supportive family. I really wanted for nothing materially. We were comfortable enough; we had two cars and a foreign holiday most years. I was very lucky in many ways. I look back now to see that I was 'privileged'. I had a good circle of close friends, a nice school I could walk to, and we lived in a village with easy access to the countryside for walking and cycling. I was also taught the value of money and that it 'didn't grow on trees'! I wouldn't have changed my childhood. On second thought, maybe I would; if I could wave a magic wand, I would have wished for more children in my community to have looked like me and for there to have been some teachers at my school from more diverse heritages. That would have been amazing.

Looking back, I realise that I didn't see myself represented anywhere, not at school among the children or teachers (who were such role models), not in my community, not in children's books, and hardly ever on the television or in magazines—where was I?

I was an avid reader growing up. One of my favourite series of books was *Malory Towers* by Enid Blyton from the 1940s. I wished I, too, could go to boarding school; it sounded wonderful. In reality, I may well have hated it.

In later life, at university, I met many people that had gone to boarding school, and some really disliked it. It wasn't all picnics, open-water swimming, lacrosse, and ginger beer, as they'd have us believe in those Enid Blyton stories! Reading those books shaped me. I wanted to be in those stories and live that life, but I was not a main or even a subsidiary character in those stories; I didn't feature. I wasn't ever sure where I would fit in while growing up. What could I be when I was older? Did I feel I had to overcompensate? People please? Maybe. Perhaps I had to work harder to 'fit in'. As human beings, we all want to feel a sense of 'belonging'.

I have always loved my brown skin, the look of it, the smooth feel of it, and the way it glows in the sunshine. If I am honest, I have had an on/off love affair with my afro hair over the years. As a very young child with my little curly afro in the 1970s, I didn't really think about it. Then, I remember, at about age seven or eight, I wanted to have hair like my friends' that flowed in the breeze. I used to run up and down the garden with a towel or a pair of tights on my head and pretend I had hair that flowed as all of my friends' hair did. As I grew into my later teens, I learned to love it and all the different things I could do with it, and I enjoyed trying out a lot of different styles.

Growing up in a white majority culture, as I didn't see myself portrayed in society as beautiful, at times, I questioned whether my features were actually beautiful: my hair, my nose. In those awkward teenage years of first kisses, I remember worrying that the boys might not want to kiss me as they wouldn't think I was beautiful. After all, I was 'different'. I wasn't like the girls/ladies on the magazine covers in the shops and all of the other girls in my class. So, although I liked my Caribbean features, I felt as if society didn't value my 'different' looks. The lack of diverse representation in the media affected my confidence growing up as I did not fit the image of what was held as 'beautiful'.

At about the age of thirteen or fourteen, I grew more curious and interested in my Caribbean cultural heritage, and I was fortunate enough to go on my first trip to Jamaica with my wonderful Great Aunty Emily. I stayed for a month in my dad's old home, where he grew up, in the countryside, in an area called Sweetland. It was so beautiful and a wonderfully rich experience for me. There were tropical fruit trees all around the house: orange, grapefruit, mango, avocado, pear, and many more. After the old Jamaican tradition, each child born in 'Francis Yard' had a fruit tree planted for them in the 'yard'. To Jamaicans, the 'yard' is the garden. I remember looking out over 'Francis yard'. It stretched out over the hilltop as far as the eye could see. The fruit and vegetables grew so well under the constant sunshine and richly fertile soil that it was a lush scene all around. On that visit, I met my granddad for the first time and all of my extended family out there. It was a wonderfully enriching trip, and I have many happy memories of it. I loved it; life felt easy and relaxed there. I felt connected to my extended family, cultural heritage, and ancestors, too.

Although I did experience a 'cultural disconnect' from my Caribbean roots growing up in such 'white' areas in my everyday life, I was able to connect to Jamaica on extended holidays and when we met up with my dad's side of the family for celebrations.

That was my experience. Many years later, it felt as though history was repeating itself when my own daughter, then aged eight or nine, started bemoaning her curly (completely gorgeous) hair, wishing it was straight like her friends' hair. Hearing her talk about it reminded me of my own feelings growing up and how I used to wear the towels and tights on my head to feel the swish.

It made me reflect on my experiences growing up and feeling different, and hers, too. I felt as though we needed to start to really celebrate and embrace our differences—our curly hair—even if Western society wasn't. Why should she want to be something else? Why did we value one hair type above another? Why did I want to be something that I wasn't? We have really embraced it since then and have enjoyed styling her hair in so many different ways, with plaits, braids, twists, and so on. That was many years ago, before I became poorly with my breast cancer, but the thought was lodged in my mind then, before I started on my own journey of post-traumatic growth, the search for my identity, and embracing my differences. I didn't want my daughter to grow up feeling negative about her 'differences' but empowered and positive about them.

A couple of years after my cancer treatment, after I'd felt so low and had a soul-searching experience, thinking about how it was important for me on a personal level to really embrace what made me 'different', I had an epiphany, a moment of clarity, the desire to make a change and a difference. I realised that I needed to turn the 'I'm different' feeling from a negative into a positive for my own sake, my daughter's, and anyone else who'd ever had the feeling of not belonging due to their being 'different' or not being 'enough'.

Emboldened by my recent near death experience, the fact that we only have one life was at the forefront of my mind. Once I'd recovered from the trauma of the cancer, I felt braver and had the strong desire to overcome my fears and do something new and bold. After all, we only live once.

So, what could I do to make a difference? How could I improve things? I decided to connect, learn more, and fill in the gaps my education had left in my own heritage and history. I read more books — history, fiction, and children's books — watched history programmes, and educated myself more. It was a supercharged journey of cultural self-discovery. I loved every minute of it and continue to do so. For my full reading list, see the back of my book — it's worth a look.

I founded my own organisation in August 2020, an educational consultancy organisation called *Diversity Days Everyday* to help schools and teachers to embed diversity and inclusive learning in the fabric and curriculum of our schools. I now support schools to help them weave it into the learning throughout the year rather than just tag it on during 'Black History

Month'. Going out and working with teachers and senior leadership teams in schools has been a hugely cathartic process for me. I feel as though I'm helping to put right the wrongs of my past, filling in the gaps, and creating a more inclusive educational experience for the children coming after me in which everyone's differences are valued and everyone can see themselves in their learning to see how they fit into the British story and how they belong. Teachers need to have a better understanding of Britain's Empire and our interconnected histories, which are irrevocably intertwined, so they can bring these lessons to the next generation.

I have also written copious notes and had a go at writing several children's books (it was harder than I thought!) with main characters from dual-heritage backgrounds about growing up in the UK and looking at the world through a different lens. It's a unique perspective and a voice we don't hear very much. I'm still working on these books.

I decided to completely grow out my own 'chemically treated/texturised' hair during the lockdown in 2020.

I went totally natural with my curly hair, and it felt good. It took a while to get used to looking after natural hair again and also to get used to how big it was, but I've definitely embraced it. Getting back to being 'me' — not a watered-down or 'more acceptable' version of me — has been a positive move.

I even did a DNA test in the spring of 2021; it was a fascinating experience. The results were as expected but also so interesting to actually see. I found out that I am fifty per cent English and Northwestern European, specifically from Yorkshire, East Midlands, and the Potteries, which accounts for my mother's side of the family and fits in with her understanding of her family tree. My other side is Jamaican from the 1700s onwards, stemming from my father's family. Then, going way back many hundreds of years before the 1700s, my DNA is eighteen per cent Nigerian plus eleven per cent from Benin and Togo, ten per cent Cameroon, Congo, and Western Bantu Peoples, seven per cent Ivory Coast and Ghana, two per cent from Mali, and two per cent from Ireland. I found that, genetically, I was a melting pot of genes, as most people are. Diversity makes us stronger; I believe this is true genetically and culturally. I hope one day to visit the countries of my great ancestors and explore the continent of Africa.

I joined Instagram, (re-joined) Facebook, Twitter, and LinkedIn to connect with others of similar interests, backgrounds, and/or cultural heritages, and that has been an amazingly positive experience. Through these social media platforms, I have made some new 'real' connections and also managed to reconnect with long-lost old friends from my very early childhood, which was magical. I avoided social media for years, only thinking of the bad things that might come with it, but with careful personal boundaries and limits, it can be an amazing resource when harnessed for good, helping you find your 'tribe'. I could hardly believe it when, one day, I found a Twitter group that 'amplifies space for mixed-race/multi-heritage teachers' called '@_MixEdUK' to share their unique experiences — so niche, and so me! I don't think I've ever found a group where I've felt as if it was so made for me.

By listening to my inner voice, with support, I've been able to unpack my burdens and baggage and truly embrace and celebrate my differences, turning what was once a source of pain into a shining light of hope for the future on a personal and wider level. Reconnecting with my inner self has given me deeper roots and wings.

On a personal level, it has been a truly cathartic process to unearth what I'd buried so deeply inside me, to shine a light on it, and allow it to blossom, bloom, and thrive.

We each have our own stories of our childhoods, and these early, formative years leave an imprint on us as we grow into adulthood.

Reflect...

This was my very personal journey of self-discovery, and ultimately, of growth. What's yours? It will be so different for each of us as we are all as unique as our own experiences.

It makes sense to me to know that, at certain points, as we go through the journey of life, we need to stop every now and then to take stock of where we are, where we are going, and where we've been. We need to reflect on what might be troubling us and re-evaluate our lives, relationships, jobs, and careers, and allow ourselves to make changes and grow.

CHAPTER 8

Connection of Mind and Body

The inter-connectedness of the mind and the body is something I think I've always been aware of. The benefits of getting 'out' of our heads and being more in touch with our bodies—through physical sensations, gentle stretching, yoga, Pilates, gardening, walking, and swimming; really, any physical activity that floats your boat is good.

When your body feels good, your mind also feels good, and vice versa, be it calm, excited, or joyful.

When our minds are calm and relaxed, that, in turn, sends a signal to our bodies not to hold onto tension but to let it go, and we physically unwind.

However, if we are emotionally tense or stressed, we also hold that tension in our bodies, which can lead to other health problems. Holding tension in our faces, our jawlines, our necks, and our shoulders are classic. I have also experienced, after prolonged periods of exhaustion and/or tiredness, a feeling of generalised aches and pains all over my body, particularly in my neck, back, and shoulders. It's an ever-present ache, sometimes with sharp, pin-pricking pains, too. I am all too aware that this is brought on by my mind not being in a good place, feeling stressed, or overly worrying about something.

Our feelings and emotions come and go, depending on the stresses and strains in our everyday lives. I generally feel very in touch with my mind and body connection. I feel as though I listen to the signals my body gives me and respond to them. However, as we approached Christmas 2018, I tried to ignore signs of stress in my body. I ignored the aches and pains, my sore head (I don't normally suffer from headaches), and the dizziness, and then I was tearful and cried every day as I drove home from work. Then, when I started bursting into tears uncontrollably at work, I could no longer ignore it. The signs that I wasn't well were getting stronger and stronger. I felt fragile, vulnerable, on edge, and at the breaking point. I had no choice but to stop and press 'pause' for a bit.

'Embrace and love your body, it is the most amazing thing you will ever own.'
—*Patrick Hutchinson*

I think I owe it to myself—and you owe it to yourself, too—to take good care of yourself. We only have one life; it's a gift. We get one body—let's look after it.

When our bodies and minds go through a trauma, we get through it as we have to keep pushing through. There is a focus to it, and I hope we can see an end to it and we can often gain access to support during this intense time. For many of us, our brains automatically go into coping mode and focus on getting through it. It's often after the event when the critical phase of the stress has passed, the support is reduced or has stopped, and the exhaustion of the ordeal has set in, that we allow ourselves to let our guard down. That is often when we feel at our worst and are no longer coping. It is a perfect storm of tiredness and an 'Oh, my goodness, what just happened there?' realisation takes place. You reflect on the rollercoaster journey you have just taken and begin the long journey of processing what has happened on a physical and psychological level, too.

This is, I believe, the perfect time to reconnect with our bodies and allow the time and space to heal and restore and renew ourselves. I found gentle exercise so beneficial. Also, being outside and exercising was a real tonic, so gardening and walking and talking with my friend out over the fields around where we live was so restorative.

Reconnecting with your body by taking a regular hot bath and massaging some nice body cream all over you afterwards is such a nice, simple, relaxing treat, a real little pamper session. It doesn't take long or cost much, but the benefits are huge.

I suppose it's also about 'self-love', valuing yourself enough to devote the time to do what you want to do. Giving yourself permission to spend some quality time on yourself feels amazing, I have to say. Putting yourself first for a little bit of the day is good for you; it fills your cup.

Take some time to reconnect with your physical body in different ways — exercising, pampering time, quiet meditation time — and see what you like best. There is no wrong or right to this; it's whatever makes you feel good.

After a stressful time, our minds may be used to overly worrying. This can become rumination, going over and over something in your head but not really getting anywhere.

A Helpful Hint

The good thing to know is that our minds are 'elastic', and they can be retrained. Like water down a pile of sand, our thoughts travel down the path of least resistance, the one most frequently and recently travelled. So, if you've been mainly preoccupied with worrying—perhaps related to a recent health issue or some other tragedy that has befallen yourself or a loved one—your mind will get used to travelling down that path of worry and rumination. Even after the stressful event has passed, you may continue to worry or feel generally anxious or unsafe. At that point, it helps us to become aware of how our brains, minds, and thoughts work. Knowledge of this can bring hope.

I learned that new neural pathways could be created over time through positive experiences and thoughts. Our neural pathways are a series of connected neurons that send signals from one part of the brain to another. Basically, our brains are elastic—they can be moulded, shaped, and retrained to think in different ways. This optimistic reality was once shared by the CBBC show *Operation Ouch*, when they explained to young children how their brains, minds, and thoughts work. Ruby Wax also talks about this a lot in her book about Neuroplasticity, *Frazzled*. It can give hope when your thoughts are bleak, your confidence is low, and you are longing for a positive thought to start to flow.

CHAPTER 9

The Power of Nature to Restore and Replenish

B eing outside in nature makes us feel good. I like being outside and in nature's greenery. I feel at home in the countryside, although when I was in my late teens and early twenties, I loved the buzz of the city, firstly, Derby (where I grew up) and later, Glasgow (where I went to university), with the nightlife, fun, shops, and the hustle and bustle. As an adult, I am very much at home, living in a greener, leafy, rural environment as I did in my childhood.

I've always loved walking with our dogs over fields, along quiet country lanes, and over hills. A walkout (even before the daily lockdown walk!) was very much a part of my normal routine. I felt the genuine benefits of it, and I still do today.

If I'm honest, there were times when I was particularly low and I even struggled to get out of the house. I withdrew into myself and found it hard to see anyone outside of my immediate family. It didn't last too long—a few days—but during those times, I lay on the sofa in a sort of meditative state, unable to watch telly or focus on a book. I would just rest, look out of the window, and watch the sun dance about on the foliage of the garden, the willow tree, and the flowering cherry bush. I saw wild birds come and go and noticed how the wind blew the trees. The view of nature from our window sometimes inspired me to create something from it—a drawing, a painting, or a little bit of hand-sewing. I found that a bit of creative time could be therapeutic and a positive distraction.

There have been many studies showing the therapeutic benefits, both mental and physical, of being outside in nature. There are also studies that show the benefits of simply putting one foot in front of the other and walking to realign your brain after a trauma or stressful event. Walking outside can be a simple and effective way of alleviating stress and helping to restore yourself from a persistently low mood. The ancient Japanese practice of 'forest bathing'—spending time in forests and woodlands and taking in the experience using all your senses—is growing in popularity around the world. The sights, sounds, and smells of being in the forest are a cleansing balm to the soul. It's another way to restore and replenish yourself.

So, getting out into the green, looking up at the blue sky and white clouds to purposefully notice the subtle changes in the seasons—the trees, hedgerows, bushes, flowers, and so on—is all good for us.

It's good for your mind to really look to observe what you see. There has been, in recent years, much talk of 'mindfulness' and the health benefits of being in the moment. Children are so natural and good at that. The number of times my children have spotted something while out and about before me! Children are naturally 'in the moment', and that's the joy of them. As adults, we start to live more and more in our 'heads', always thinking about what has passed or planning what's to come. The more we can train our brains to focus and enjoy what's in front of us, the better. Nature, I think, makes that easy because, in nature, there is always something to observe and something beautiful to marvel at.

When I was unwell, I often borrowed my friend's gorgeous dog, Skye, for a walk and a cuddle. I found that a good thing for both my body and my soul. It was a chance for some fresh air, walking out over the beautiful countryside with stunning scenery and views for miles. After the walk, I'd often sit on my friend's kitchen floor for a bit, fussing over the dog and looking into her big eyes. It filled my soul. Animals, especially dogs, show such uncomplicated, unconditional affection and love to those they know well, which is priceless and such a tonic to a troubled soul. I have heard of many accounts of people suffering from poor mental health, such as depression, who have found solace in spending time with a dog. They can be real lifesavers for some, a reason to get up, get out, and keep going, and their sense of loyalty is wonderful. You can create such a tight bond with a dog. This brings to mind Ricky Gervais's excellent series 'Afterlife', in which a depressed man manages to stay alive, in part, because of his responsibility to his dog.

After enjoying walking my friend's dog so much, after writing the word 'dog' on my notes of inspiration that brought me joy, it was inevitable that we, too, would get a family dog of our own.

Due to unforeseen circumstances (i.e., the global pandemic and our UK lockdown), we ended up getting our own puppy sooner rather than later. The time felt right, and we knew we would have enough time to devote to the early stages of puppy training. We got Rocco, our border collie puppy, in mid-March of 2020, and he's been amazing. We all love him so much, and he's brought so much richness to our lives. Having animals to pet and stroke reduces our stress levels, which is why we are hearing of the popularity of therapy dogs these days.

A few months later, we did what we'd been thinking of doing for ages: we rescued two gorgeous kittens, a brother and sister, Beau and Willow, from a local cat shelter. We also got four chickens. Now we have our own menagerie, and the house and garden are full of life, like a mini-farm. It brings us a lot of joy.

So, along with being out in nature and enjoying it, and spending therapeutic time with animals, we can also embrace nature's bounty as the seasons roll on and enjoy what she provides for us free: wild garlic in March, elderflower cordial in May, strawberries in August, blackberries and blackcurrants in September, and all the tree fruit — apples, pears, plums to name but a few.

Also, if time, space, and energies allow, there's the fun of sowing seeds in early spring for home-grown vegetables and flowers that can be brought inside. All of these activities connect us to nature and the world around us, which takes us out of our heads and into the present moment, which is good for our mental health.

A Helpful Hint

Get out into the fresh air as much as you can when you can and engage with nature—it will help to uplift and improve your mood—but don't feel bad when you can't due to time or energy levels.

CHAPTER 10

Relationships

Trauma takes its toll on you and your loved ones. If you are the one who experiences a stressful situation firsthand, then you will undoubtedly be affected by the event. The impact will depend on the severity of the trauma and its duration, your prior life experiences, and your personality.

You may experience all or some of the following:

- a sense of numbness or loss of connection with your emotions — this is your body's form of self-protection (detachment);
- tension and muscular aches, especially in the neck and shoulders;

- tiredness, fatigue, lethargy, and possibly insomnia;
- intrusive memories or thoughts;
- sadness, feelings of depression or tearfulness; and/or
- withdrawal, wanting to retreat into yourself and avoid company.

I personally experienced all of these to some degree. I went through this period post-treatment (six months later), and I felt like a very different 'me'. I felt vulnerable, withdrawn, and quiet; my confidence was at rock bottom, and due to all of the worrying, I also felt tired and generally lethargic. It was exhausting. It was a very difficult time for my family and me, especially as, at my lowest point, I found myself bursting into tears out of the blue, which our children found most distressing, I think. During the actual treatment, I managed to 'cope', so my family wasn't unduly worried or upset about me. The worry set in for all of us after, as it was very clear that I had a lot to process emotionally.

The Derby Royal Hospital gave me a very helpful booklet by the Nottinghamshire Healthcare NHS Foundation Trust called *Coping with the Effects of a Traumatic Event* that described a helpful analogy. It talked about how, when you experienced a trauma, you had to deal with it at the moment. You experienced a range of emotions and thoughts you are unable to deal with at the time, such as fear, worry, shock, guilt, numbness, and so on.

As a result, these feelings are packed in an imaginary bag and taken away from the moment of the trauma. However, this 'emotional luggage', because it has been so badly packed and in a rush, frequently bursts open, especially when it is 'knocked' against something. This is often experienced as distressing thoughts, images, and feelings that are pushed out of our minds as they are too upsetting.

Over a period of time, we unpack and repack this 'emotional baggage' and try to make sense of our emotions and feelings in an attempt to process what has happened. In the end, we manage to get rid of some items, such as guilt and anger, and rearrange others, which may result in having a different perspective when we look back on our experiences. This process of unpacking and repacking our 'emotional baggage' is a painful one, but it does become easier.

The hope is that, eventually, the bag stops bursting open unexpectedly, and we are able to look into that emotional bag or revisit the trauma without it causing undue distress. Eventually, the bag feels so light that we will hardly notice we are carrying it at all.

As I said at the start of this chapter, trauma takes its toll on the person directly experiencing it and their loved ones, too. We decided, as parents, to be as open and honest with our children as we could. We decided to tell them whatever they needed to know in terms of my diagnosis, treatment, and long road of emotional and physical recovery on a 'need to know' basis. I couldn't hide my tears from them at home; I didn't want to put on a front and pretend everything was normal. Children are so astute, able to pick up on emotions and tiny signs in the house. I didn't want them putting two and two together and coming up with six. So, we had to talk about it as a family and explain what was going on. They were still young—nine and seven years old—and it was hard, but they were both amazing. I know it was distressing and unsettling for them to see their mummy so upset, but as we explained, 'this is life', with its ups and downs. At that moment, I wasn't at my best, but I was going to get better with time and the right help. So, although it was initially confusing for them to see me upset, they were able to deal with it, and more importantly, they knew it was not their fault (sometimes children blame themselves when something goes 'wrong' in the family).

I was very lucky to have such good support around me in my immediate family. My parents were a constant source of strength, practical help, and a listening ear. My mum found it particularly hard to see me so unhappy and suffering emotionally for so long that, at times, she didn't know what to say to me. She was frightened of saying the wrong thing. Her natural inclination was distraction and business at times like that, so a lot of cooked meals and baking came our way! We are all different, and my dad was able to sit with the uncomfortableness of the feelings and just listen, talk, and support me emotionally. We all have different skill sets, and together, they made a great support team.

My husband was an absolute rock. He was truly amazing during that difficult time in our lives. He was there every step of the way, supporting me, and on a practical level, he took over the running of the house for many months, including the cooking, cleaning, washing, and so on, at the same time as doing his full-time job. He had an amazing capacity to take on the extra workload and look after his family, emotionally and practically. I will be forever grateful to him for that, for keeping the ship afloat, and I love him for it.

It did, however, take its toll on him, of course, but he bottled it up as I was too unwell to share it with. The strain he was under was too much at times. I think I had a small idea of what he was going through, but I was so absorbed in sorting myself out that I had no capacity to see much outside of my own problems. As I gradually started to come up and out of my low mood, my husband started to unpack and repack his emotional bag, which was painful for both of us, but it was good to talk about. In one conversation, we even 'deconstructed' the social construct of marriage and questioned whether marriage was even possible or a good idea. We decided 'yes' in the end; we wouldn't want to be without each other.

Relationships and marriage are not just for the good, fun, easy times; they are also for the tough times when you are going through a storm. We certainly went through a tough time, and it put a real strain on our relationship, but we came through the storm together, becoming stronger and pulling tightly together.

After talking about it, I reflected that our relationship was like a plant (subconsciously, I think this might have come from my uncle, Jeffrey, who is a minister, and who said it to us at our wedding ceremony). They need care and attention, or they will wither and die. They can cope with a little neglect for some time but not too long. The more we nurture our love, the more it thrives. So, I think we should nurture our loved ones and let them nurture us, too. Treasure them. Tend to them like a plant, little and often. Be honest. Be open. Take care of each other.

Reflect...

In our families and our relationships, it's okay to be vulnerable. You don't have to play the part of being the 'strong' one, as I used to think was my role to play, always okay, in control, coping, and being brave for everyone else.

As my friend, Lynne, says, in our families, we can all take turns at being 'held' by the others and being looked after. Families are there to support one another.

CHAPTER 11

Brave, Not Perfect!

As a part of my recovery process, the 'unpacking' and 'repacking', I found myself reassessing some of my ideas about life and my approach to it.

I asked myself some questions: Do I feel fulfilled? What do I most want to do in life? What do I want to achieve? What was holding me back from reaching for my dreams? What was I afraid of? I mused, pondered, and reflected on these questions. I read some books and did some more thinking, and concluded that, perhaps, I had always put too much pressure on myself to do everything perfectly. Where had that pressure come from? Society? Me? Was it the same for boys, too, or was the phenomenon particular to girls? Were boys taught to be 'brave' and girls taught to be 'perfect'? I read *Brave, Not Perfect* by Reshma Saujani; it was a great read, and it altered my outlook on life. It was interesting, inspiring, and liberating, too. It made me realise it's okay to have a go and for it not to work out. Also, you don't have to be great at something before you try it. Before, I might not have tried things I wasn't sure I was really good at for fear of 'failing'.

I felt braver, bolder, and unencumbered by a worrying sense of 'what if it all goes wrong?' It was a great feeling; 'better to have tried and not succeeded than to have never tried at all' was my new motto. Put more simply: brave, not perfect. My husband often reminds me of this saying now, particularly when I have a wobble about doing something new and feel a bit nervous. I find it really helps me.

I also remember a head teacher at school once saying, 'Don't ever be in a position at the end of your days, rocking in your chair, thinking '*What if?*' Basically, she was saying to us that we should pursue our dreams and live our lives to the fullest before it was too late.

This thought spurs me on to have a go in life, follow my passions, and try to make a difference when it comes to things I care about. What drives me is the desire to make positive changes for myself, my family, my friends, my community, and beyond, to make our world a better place. It's what keeps me going.

Bravery and courage are not the absence of fear; it is feeling fearful but doing it anyway.

CHAPTER 12

Embrace the New You!

Here we are, at the beginning of the final chapter of this book, but an end is also a new beginning, a new chapter of the new you—dare to be your amazing self!

I learnt as I went on my journey of self-healing that I was certainly a changed person from who I was before. Initially, I was sort of in 'mourning' for the former me, the me without the cancer diagnosis, the treatment, the invasive surgery, the upset, the worry, and the trauma. I missed the fun, being carefree, the easy, relaxed me, the it'll-be-okay me. Having been through what I had, I didn't recognise myself anymore, and I found that upsetting and challenging. I remember feeling as if it might be hard to be with my friends if I wasn't the 'normal' me they knew; if I wasn't fun, happy, and jokey like I used to be. This made me question why I felt as if it was hard to show people my real emotions. Maybe I thought that some people wouldn't like me if I wasn't fun to be with.

I had to learn to be comfortable with the 'new me', the real, authentic me who had been through physical, emotional, and psychological trauma and survived. I felt it hard to embrace the 'new me' as I preferred the 'old me'. My psychologist said, 'I like this Clare,' and it was so lovely to hear her say that as she was accepting me just as I was.

That was when my psychologist introduced me to the idea of the Japanese bowl. I needed to start telling myself a new story, giving myself a fresh, new, positive perspective. It helped me so much on my journey that I embraced the new story, and consequently, the new me, too.

Kintsugi is the centuries-old Japanese art of fixing broken pottery. The word roughly translates to 'golden joinery', and it shows that, for the Japanese, the value of an object is not in its beauty but in its imperfections, and these imperfections were something to celebrate, not hide.

Rather than re-join broken ceramic pieces with a camouflaged adhesive, the Kintsugi technique uses a special tree sap lacquer dusted with powdered gold, silver, or platinum. Once completed, the beautiful seams of gold shine in the cracks of the pottery pieces.

This special method celebrates each artefact's unique history by emphasising its fractures and breaks instead of hiding or disguising them. In fact, Kintsugi often makes the repaired piece even more beautiful and valuable than the original, and they are extremely collectable in Japanese culture.

In 2010, Peter Mayer wrote a beautiful song about this called 'Japanese Bowl'. It's worth searching for and listening to. In the lyrics, he likens himself to a Japanese bowl, broken, now repaired, and more valuable and special. It helps us to see the beauty in our imperfect journeys in life. It helped me to look back on the journey I'd just experienced in a new light.

This ancient Japanese philosophy and practice helped me see the beauty in my imperfections and embrace my new, imperfect, authentic self. The new me had learned so much as a result of what I'd been through. I knew myself better. I was now much kinder to myself and had been able to put practical strategies into place to help myself get well again with support.

I now feel stronger, more resilient, and better prepared for the ups and downs of life. I also feel so much braver in my approach to life. With my own eyes, I have seen that life is short. You never know when your time might be up, so we might as well make the most of it while we can.

So, grab life by the horns, enjoy the ride, and remember to be kind to yourself and others along the way.

As one of my best friends at university used to say,

"It will all be all right in the end...and if it's not quite all right...you're not quite at the end yet!"
—*Melissa Thompson*

When the road of life gets tough, hold on—better days will come. Get support if you need it, and reach out to people who can help you. There is no shame in feeling as though you are not coping in life. Be open, be honest, be kind to yourself, and give yourself time. You will be okay.

A Letter to the Reader

Mrs Clare Francis-Slater
Derbyshire

Dear Reader with a Broken Soul,

Above all, don't worry.

Even though life feels hard at the moment, these tough times will pass. Every storm cloud runs out of rain. The sun will shine on you again.

Until then, take good care of yourself. Doing so makes you feel better. Sleep and eat well, get into nature, and get daily fresh air and exercise. Treat yourself to long hot soaks in the bath (if you like them) or hot showers! If you like animals, spend time with them, enjoy time without doing much, and don't feel guilty about being unproductive. Connect with loved ones and friends, enjoy some quiet time alone, and be kind to yourself. Think about what brings you joy and do it. Try to take the pressure off yourself. Make plans to do nice things, but hold these plans lightly,and be grateful for what you have by always counting your blessings.

*I hope my **Little Book of Balm** has been of some comfort to you.*

Reach out for help if you need it.

Remember that you are not alone.

With warmest wishes,

Clare xxx

A Final Thought

As the seasons come and go, observe and enjoy the changes they bring.

Notice the buds of new growth in spring. Bask in the summer's sun. Relax and read a good book. Stretch! Notice the beautiful colour changes in autumn and enjoy the fruit of the season. Be snuggly in the winter, and make the most of being cosy indoors: fire on, blankets on laps, hot water bottles in bed, hot chocolate with whisky cream, candles inside, and twinkly lights outside. Gather friends around for coffee and cake as often as you can.

All of these things can make us feel good and promote positive mental health. Add to this list and do whatever makes you feel good!

Go well (as my psychologist, Kirsty, used to say to me upon parting at the end of each session).

Notes

Notes

Notes

Notes

Notes

Notes

About the Author

*Clare Francis-Slater MAHons, PGCE, QTS, CELTA, Founder
of Diversity Days Everyday and Tra La La Singing Supply*

Clare Francis-Slater lives in Derbyshire with her family, husband, two children, dog, two cats, and chickens, and is a skilled and experienced teacher, educational consultant, lecturer, and writer. She has taught mainly in primary schools and other educational settings for over twenty years. She is now a freelancer and associate lecturer at The University of Derby.

Clare is also the founder of an educational consultancy organisation, *Diversity Days Everyday.* The aim of the organisation is to support the embedding of diversity in schools so that every child growing up in the UK can see themselves in their educational experience, feel valued, and understand how they fit into the history of Britain.

She started to write this book after having been diagnosed with breast cancer in 2018 and recovering. It was the kind of book she would have wanted to read to support her recovery and help her cope with the trauma she experienced.

After Clare recovered from her cancer treatment, she went on an uplifting personal journey that helped her embrace her 'whole' self and take on new and exciting projects and challenges.

hello@diversity-days.co.uk
www.diversity-days.co.uk
Twitter: *@CFrancisSlater*
Instagram: *clarefrancisslater*
Linkedin: *Clare Francis-Slater*

Bibliography

The following list of books helped steady me in uncertain times. They gave me roots (a better understanding of myself, my heritage, and history of my ancestry, how my mind works, the body-mind connection) and wings (strength to fly, go out into the world and have a go at things without fear of failure, which is so important).

Books about self-care, healing the mind and body and challenging patterns of thinking...

- **Seeking Slow,** Melanie Barnes
- **Pause,** Danielle Marchant
- **Brave not Perfect,** Reshma Saujani
- **You are Awesome,** Matthew Syed
- **How to be Human,** Ruby Wax
- **Self-care for the Real World,** Nadia Narain & Katia Narain Phillips
- **Love for Imperfect Things,** Haemin Sunim
- **The book of Hygge,** Louisa Thomsen Brits
- **The Wild Remedy,** Emma Mitchell
- **Rest,** Alex Soojung-Kim Pang

Books that fed my thirst for learning, filling in the gaps in my understanding of a wider more inclusive British and world history...

- **The entire collection of Andrea Levy's books; The Long Song 1800-1850, Six Stories and an Essay 1914, Small Island 1930–1950, Every Light in the House Burning 1952–1958, Never far from Nowhere 1960–1970, Fruit of the Lemon 1972–1982,** Andrea Levy
- **The Hill we Climb,** Amanda Gorman
- **Purple Hibisiscus, Half of a Yellow Moon,** Chimamanda Ngozi Adichie
- **Girl, Woman, Other,** Bernadine Evaristo
- **Taking up Space,** Chelsea Kwayke and Ore Ogunbiyi
- **500 Words, Black Lives Matter,** a moving compilation of poetry written by children in response to BLM movement, their own voices being heard.
- **Why I'm no longer taking ... about Race,** Reni Eddo-Lodge
- **Natives,** Akala

- **A Little guide for teachers, Diversity in Schools,** Bennie Kara

... and last, but not least .... A complete powerhouse of a book and an essential read for all:

- **Black and British,** David Olusoga

With Greatest Thanks to...

All of my gorgeous family: Ben, my rock, my beautiful children, Amelia and Theo, who were amazing beyond their years, and my mum and my dad, who are always there for me with never-ending love and support. Thank you to Angela and Emily, the best sis and sister-in-law ever, for supporting me from the sidelines, only a phone call away!

And my friends—you know who you are—who kept scooping me up when I needed it most and were there for me. Clare Brown, thank you so much. You were a constant source of support and a listening ear when I dipped. All of the dog walks and talks really helped me recover. Also, Trudi and Rhian—thanks for the chats and cups of tea in the garden, the endless understanding and fun spa days!

Lindy (Cindy-Louise/Sleeping Beauty!), thanks for your trainers (you know what I mean!), your boundless joy, love of life, energy, and fun, and for crying with me on the beach after a cocktail or two and sharing and connecting so openly with my heritage on our amazing adventure in Jamaica!

Mary Lewis, for your serenity and calm aura. Thank you for being such a kind friend.

Donna, thank you for your kindness and support and for being your lovely self. And to your friend, Clare, for her helpful feedback on my manuscript. I do appreciate our deep chats (I think we should have a podcast, just saying!). I love your perspective and sense of humour. I feel like I'm on Radio 4 when we talk together.

Lisa Singleton, for scooping me up 'that day' when I needed to not be on my own and a shoulder to cry on and someone to open my heart to. Thank you for being there.

Beth Burrows, for our days out and walks and talks around stately homes and gardens, countless cups of tea and slices of cake! It is always a pleasure!

Denisa, you have always inspired me. You are a powerhouse of energy with a 'can-do' attitude! I think you're amazing.

Rachel Ford and Kathy Riches, for being your completely lovely selves! I wish I saw you both more!

Thank you to Kate Taylor for giving me a gentle nudge to do and be more than I ever thought I could. You gave me courage when I felt wobbly and unsure if I could do the work I was doing. Thank you!

Thank you to all my neighbours for being lovely! Having lovely neighbours helps!

Thank you to Jackie, my school friend, who created a professional looking website for my consultancy organisation. You are so talented, and it was so lovely to work and re-connect with a good old friend.

To Caroline, my old school friend, for reading my manuscript. For your positivity, support, and encouragement.

To Sarah Cheadle, for being a constant, loyal friend from the beginning.

Thank you to my Jamaican family here and abroad, for helping me to stay connected to my roots. I love you all.

Thank you to my friend and creative partner, Lynne Hollingsworth, for supporting all of my creative endeavours and being one of my biggest cheerleaders. I have always loved working with you on a project, and this project has been no exception. Here's to many more!

Thank you to all of the amazing staff and schoolteachers that I've worked with in and around Derbyshire and Derby, and to Claire's School Solutions Teaching Agency for the huge support you have given me, both on my book-writing journey and my consultancy work with *Diversity Days Everyday*. I felt seen, heard, and valued.

Thank you to Daniella Blechner, my book journey mentor and publisher. You helped give shape to my ideas and the time and space to allow me to create my own book. I could not have done this without your guidance, support, editing, and know-how! Your patience and encouragement have enabled me to make this happen. Thank you so much from the bottom of my heart.

Thank you, Baasit Siddiqui and Dr Nichola Trudi Felicia Jones for your kind words. I appreciate you both reading my book and for your support of it.

Conscious Dreams
PUBLISHING

Transforming diverse writers
into successful published authors

www.consciousdreamspublishing.com

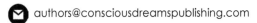
authors@consciousdreamspublishing.com

Let's connect